A Summer Place

A Summer Place

Living by the Sea

Tricia Foley

RIZZOLI
NEW YORK

New York · Paris · London · Milan·

TABLE OF CONTENTS

OPPOSITE: A white canvas umbrella and painted table and chairs set the scene for outdoor living.

INTRODUCTION

The village comes to life on Saturday morning, when people head to the ferry for the beach or the farm stand for their provisions. Bicycles come out from behind the hedges on Bellport Lane and friends stop to visit and catch up on the week and make plans for the weekend. Dinners are booked, movies are scheduled, and kids' playdates organized. But the summer season actually starts Friday evening, when most of the weekenders come out and head to a favorite restaurant for dinner or a seat at the bar, greeting friends and neighbors and enjoying a fresh seafood plate or pizza, with glasses of rosé on every table. This is summer in Bellport.

Bellport, a small village located on the South Shore of Long Island, with Brookhaven hamlet and East Patchogue on either side, has been a destination for New Yorkers since the 1870s. With a quiet harbor as the focal point and Fire Island's barrier beach across the bay, it is naturally landscaped with sea grasses and soft, sandy beaches, and has been a subject for many painters over the years. Originally a mid-nineteenth-century whaling port, it evolved into a summer resort in the late 1800s, when the coastline was dotted with grand hotels and whitewashed boarding houses for summer visitors. Sailing was the main attraction, and sailing yachts went back and forth across the bay in regattas. Residents and visitors went to the beaches for bathing on the oceanside and attended lobster luncheons under shady pavilions. Today, strolling down Bellport Lane, with its 1840s sea captains' houses and picket fences leading down to the bay, is still a tradition.

In the late nineteenth and early twentieth centuries, residents settled in for the summer season, with some of the men commuting into the city by rail during the week. But today, although some residents come out all year long, others have settled here full time. The historical society has a barn museum and changing exhibitions every summer in their gallery, with lectures, book signings, and programming for all in the family. The frame shop on Main Street is kept busy with collectors who need their art framed, and home-goods shops carry the latest furnishings and hostess gifts.

Restaurants are full on the weekends and the porch at the one on the lane, where dogs are allowed and you can chat with friends as they pass by on their way to the ferry, is the choice spot for lunch. The bicycle shop is always busy, and Saturday morning rituals take place at the natural food store or the chic home emporium on Main Street—a purveyor of easy foods for entertaining or taking on a picnic. At three farm stands news is exchanged, dates are made, and the freshest fruits, vegetables, honey, and baked goods are bought for the weekend. And whether it's a private cocktail party or a benefit event, many partygoers arrive by bicycle in sundresses and bow ties, going through hedges to see friends.

Many residents are in creative fields and have made houses and gardens that reflect their aesthetic, and we've captured some of their inspirational design ideas for casual summer living in this book—ideas that translate to homes across the country. The homeowners feel lucky to be here, as I do, and appreciate the old-fashioned summer rituals, the sense of community, and the circle of friends that make this summer place by the sea the place they want to live. —*Tricia Foley*

BY THE SEA

OPPOSITE: Bicycling is a preferred mode of transportation during summertime—
whether it's to shop at a farm stand, to visit friends, or bike to the beach.

8 A SUMMER PLACE

A HOUSE WITH A VIEW

An all white barn was the perfect next house for me. Making the transition between a compound with many small buildings to a modern barn-style dwelling tucked in the marshes with views of the sea—and in need of a makeover—was just the project I wanted. A fireplace, open-plan living, dining, and kitchen areas, and a deck that expands this living space by a third worked well for my lifestyle. After the renovation, and excluding a new dining table and bed frame, everything was brought over from my previous home and put in place: white slipcovers washed, rugs laid down, china and crystal stacked. The hardest thing was finding a place for all the books I've collected. In an extra-large bedroom, I fitted one wall with bookshelves, and the bedroom became part library, part sitting room. The square footage of the old house was comparable, but my former 1820s house was a warren of small, cozy rooms, and this 1990s house was all about tall ceiling heights and windows that open to the sky. Art from friends fills a wall gallery-style in the entrance, and the antique Belgian bench that was in my old office fits the length of the space. Friends yell up to the deck in summer to say hello when walking to the beach and stop to use the hose for water for their dogs. It felt like home right away.

PREVIOUS PAGES: My barnlike home is situated at the edge of the grassy marshland with a view of the bay. OPPOSITE: The front double door opens onto a simple wood plank platform that is punctuated by matching white painted urns. I kept the worn gray pavers leading to the door, which have settled in over the years. A pair of silver leaf maple trees provides shade and frames the entry to the house.

OPPOSITE: The entry's long wall has become a gallery space, with paintings, drawings, and photographs by mostly local artist friends. A 10-foot-long linen upholstered Belgian bench from the early 1800s grounds the art. **ABOVE AND FOLLOWING PAGES**: An open-plan kitchen and dining and living room appear more spacious with high ceilings and windows.

ABOVE, LEFT: A small gray-washed wood planter on the upstairs deck is my new kitchen herb garden, and is easy to access for snipping while cooking and when adding garnishes to my outside table setting. **RIGHT:**: Shells picked up on the beach earn their keep as salt cellars and votive holders, or, here, by holding napkins down on a breezy outdoor evening. **OPPOSITE**: In summer, the deck becomes an outdoor living room, with comfortable seating from Kingsley Bate at one end. An umbrella and large stone-topped coffee table are useful for outside entertaining. The weathered gray woods and clean white slipcovers and pillows complement the setting with its view across the marshland to the bay.

PREVIOUS PAGES: At the end of our road is a small private beach on the bay, which is the perfect place to have a supper at the water's edge. **ABOVE AND OPPOSITE**: A basket full of the essentials for a simple meal is all you need to set up, along with a few beach stones and shells to keep napkins in place.

SUMMER ENTERTAINING

SOMETIMES IT'S A COCKTAIL PARTY for fifty in summer dresses and starched white shirts and khakis, sometimes it's an intimate dinner for six, and sometimes it's a summer barbeque on the beach. But in any case, the mood is relaxed and the preparations for it should be, too.

SOME FAVORITE TABLE SETTING TIPS include using shells: clamshells with guests' names on the inside for place cards, or white votive candles, or sea salts; found scallop or oyster shells for holding down an unruly stack of napkins when it's breezy; and smaller shells and water inside candlelit hurricane shades for a nice touch on an outside table. Piling shells down the middle of the table instead of flowers creates a summery seaside centerpiece.

A CATERER'S TIP that is very welcome this season: If dining outdoors in mosquito season, spraying underneath the tables and chairs, or the hems of tablecloths, before guests come keeps the bugs away and makes it more comfortable.

ON WARM SUMMER EVENINGS, a buffet supper of farm stand salads and vegetables, pastas, or grilled fish or meat allows guests to fix their own plates, and when prepared in advance and served at room temperature, the host or hostess can be at ease to enjoy an al fresco dinner with their guests.

FOR LARGE PARTIES, there are so many options to create memorable invitations: Paperless Post, Evite, Canva. Or, use a familiar photo or child's drawing to make and send your own via email, or print and leave them rolled and tied up with raffia in neighbors' mailboxes.

NAPKINS TIED WITH RUSTIC STRING and a sprig of rosemary or thyme to hold forks and knives make silverware easier to maneuver on the buffet line. A table setting needs short, simple flowers and candles so that one can see friends across the table—small bud vases and jars work well, and a blossom or herb sprig on each plate or napkin adds a summery touch. Large flour sack towels or other checked tea towels are so much nicer and softer than stiff starched napkins for an outdoor barbecue, lobster supper, or clam bake—they're very practical, and easy to throw in the wash for next time.

LITTLE WHITE LIGHTS are not just for Christmas: they can look magical strung in the trees or shrubs to illuminate a dinner setting or define a path on the way to the party. A collection of lanterns is great to line up along a sidewalk or put on the buffet table and bar as well as on dining tables for outdoor lighting.

USE UNEXPECTED ACCESSORIES for your table setting: glass garden cloches are just the thing for displaying cheeses and keeping them fresh. A big bowl or basket of peaches or cherries adds color and looks great on the table, making the fruit ready to eat as guests linger after dinner. A few clear bottles of cool water are welcome on a hot summer evening and, adding a sprig of mint or slices of lemon or cucumber to a pitcher of water is refreshing.

OPPOSITE: It's all in the details. Simple materials, such as stones found on the beach, a piece of cheesecloth, and a sprig of rosemary from the garden, are just right for a casual summer table setting.

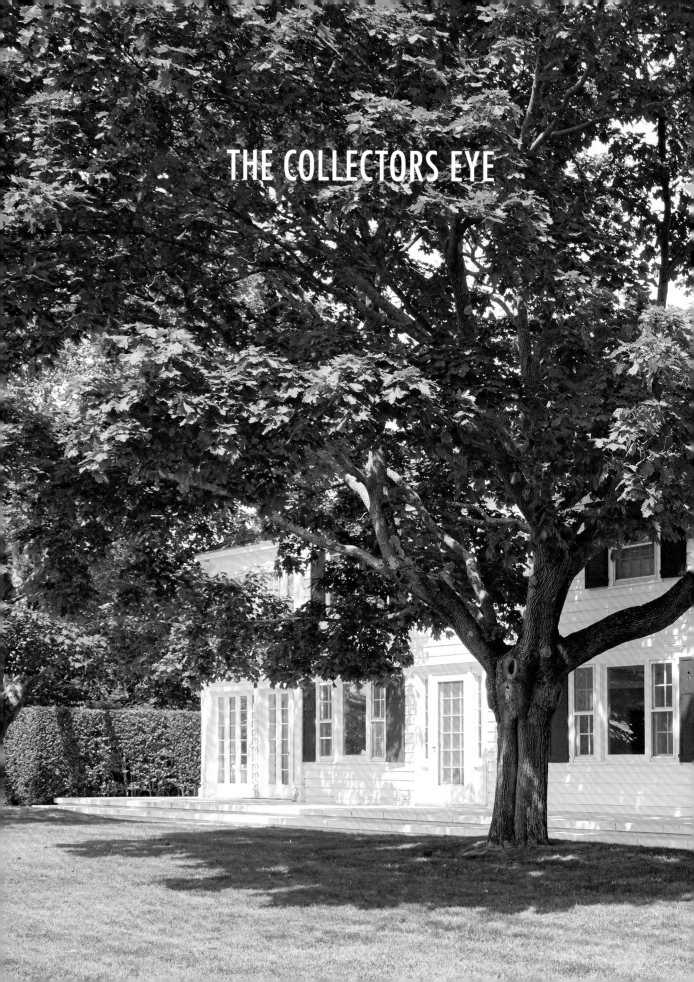

THE COLLECTORS EYE

At the end of a long pebbled drive is a quintessential white-shingled Colonial Revival Bellport house. Built in 1927, it is sited on the waterfront and has graceful hundred-year-old trees that give it a feeling of timelessness. The house was reinterpreted by architect Michael Gabellini many years ago when Sarah and Gary Wolkowitz found it—the interior was opened up, and a new sympathetic addition with a kitchen was added. All the windows and doors are original, the fireplace is restored, and the floors are refinished. The new wing sits on a platform of Bulgarian limestone slabs, seamlessly incorporating a pool, lounging and seating areas, and an outdoor grill and kitchen island.

The interiors are furnished with Christian Liaigre furniture downstairs and Armani/Casa upstairs. These simple, luxuriously shaped furnishings and materials from the owners' world travels are at home here in this all-white setting—every detail and object chosen with care and a designer's eye.

Sarah and Gary have spent most of their careers in the fashion industry and have always been collectors of fine art and photography, as evidenced in the pieces they have designed their home around. Their son, Bryce, is now a gallerist, and his children spend summer vacations here at the family compound. Their family home is a backdrop for relatives and friends, who share their table over wine, stories, and laughter.

PREVIOUS PAGES AND OPPOSITE: An allée of linden trees leads visitors down the drive to the classic white-shingled 1927 house on the water.

PREVIOUS PAGES: The living room is serene with a deep sofa and chairs from Christian Liaigre. The coffee table, with its natural wood base and glass top, was found during a vacation in Mykonos. A portrait of John Lennon by Annie Leibovitz holds pride of place here.
RIGHT: A Bulgarian limestone floor in the kitchen seamlessly opens out to the pool area. The kitchen island is Arclinea from B&B Italia. The contemporary image on the wall opposite the island is by British photographer Martin Parr.
FOLLOWING PAGES: The integration of indoors and outdoors makes the pool, lounging area, and outdoor kitchen an extended summer space for small or large gatherings.

ABOVE: A vintage Jean Prouvé table was restored and placed in the center hallway.
OPPOSITE: In the upstairs hallway, a collection of drawings by Marcel van Eeden is grouped together over a signature klismos–style bench by architect Michael Gabellini.

There are no distractions in the minimal main bedroom, with its ebony-finished platform bed and oversize lamps from Armani/Casa. The walls here, and throughout the house, are painted in Benjamin Moore's Decorator's White.

Sarah has created a shady spot overlooking the bay with a chartreuse canvas hammock for lazy afternoons and summer breezes.

ON THE BEACH

New York City architect David Ling has another life as a surfer and sailor, and he embraces every opportunity to be near the sea. His weathered wood house on Brookhaven hamlet's beachfront has views from every window of Bellport Bay, Fire Island, and the Atlantic Ocean.

This setting and the simple, natural materials used throughout make his home the quintessential beach house, with wood floors and walls, whitewashed porches, and decks equipped with state-of-the-art telescopes. In redesigning this small Cape Cod–style cottage, he increased the living space by dropping a simple rectangular box, with horizontal wood paneling weathered to match the original beach cottage shingles and white-painted trim, into the existing peaked roof. Windows take advantage of the marshland that surrounds the dwelling and provide views of the sea beyond. The pedigreed furnishings complement the minimal architecture. A small private beach, where beach chairs are always dug into the sand and his collection of surfboards and sailboats are always ready to head out on the bay, can be found across the road in front of his house.

PREVIOUS PAGES: David Ling's rooftop deck, with a guide wire railing, has an unobstructed view of the bay. OPPOSITE: The whitewashed walls and flooring of the first-floor dining area create an airy feeling. Open windows let in sea breezes. FOLLOWING PAGES: The living room is framed with a wall of floor-to-ceiling windows. The seating consists of a vintage white mid-century sofa that is flanked by a pair of Poul Kjaerholm leather lounge chairs.

ABOVE: On the first floor, a pair of mid-century modern chairs—on the left, a deep leather bucket seat with patina on a black swivel base and on the right, a natural wicker chair—reflects David's minimalist aesthetic. The vintage boat light on the wall is from his curated collection of furnishings. **OPPOSITE**: A mix of weathered wood planking on the walls and the bed platform creates visual interest in the main bedroom.

DESIGN FOR LIVING

An artist and art dealer respectively, the owners wanted their new house in Bellport to be a modern backdrop for their lives in the art world and a retreat for themselves and two grown daughters. They hired Japanese architect Toshihiro Oki to interpret their vision. The main part of the house is one level, sited in the landscape with a lawn that rolls down to the bay, and is designed to take advantage of the water views with large expanses of glass. The pool and deck are an integral part of the main floor living space, and walls inside and out are constructed with a pale brick from Denmark that is durable for the seaside construction and provides a thermal mass that heats and cools the house naturally.

The design, with its configuration of cubelike rooms, creates an easy flow between indoor and outdoor spaces and a balance of public and private spaces, making it work both for quiet weekends to recharge or for large outdoor parties with friends. The open kitchen has a stainless steel minimal island, wall-to-wall glass doors, and views of the pool and the Great South Bay. The kitchen island is usually covered with produce and native flowers from the garden. A table in the kitchen is always ready for family and friends.

PREVIOUS PAGES: For this seaside home, sited to take in the views of the bay and landscape, architect Toshihiro Oki used a pale brick on the main house with expansive glass windows. OPPOSITE: Perched on the bluff overlooking the bay, an outdoor kitchen with barbecue and kitchen appliances built into the mahagony-slatted enclosure includes banquette seating and a teak table and chairs.

ABOVE: A hallway has been outfitted with built-in wood storage closets. On the wall is Tal R's painting on paper, *A Ship Called New York*. **OPPOSITE**: Tucked into the surrounding woods on the property is a garden structure, designed and built by architects Georgia Read and Desmond Delanty, using recycled materials found at the former house that was demolished.

RIGHT: A stainless steel kitchen has doors opening to the rear lawn and the bay. **FOLLOWING PAGES**: An expansive view from the living room brings the outdoors in, and the natural travertine stone floor seen here appears throughout the house. White sofas by Vladimir Kagan, an iconic glass and wood coffee table by Noguchi, and vintage mid-century modern chairs were found at one of the local auctions and estate sales that are part of the Bellport tradition. The Elisabeth Kley ceramic vessel and a simple white paper lamp by George Nelson are perfectly at home here.

ABOVE: The museumlike setting is the ideal backdrop for the artwork that the homeowners collect, such as a Barry McGee brightly colored patchwork piece and a three-dimensional painted paper sculpture by Lynda Benglis. **OPPOSITE**: The studio is filled with drawings, paintings, and ceramic studies inspired by tree branches and natural elements from the land and sea. Architect Georgia Read designed the space, which includes work surfaces, storage, and display areas in rough-sawn cedar. **FOLLOWING PAGES**: Surrounded by sea grasses, a weathered wood-slatted structure at the water's edge serves as a guest room for friends and family.

AN OLD-FASHIONED SEASIDE GARDEN

Weekday mornings at 8 a.m., a group of women in white terry robes make their way down to the water through the shrubbery. Some walk, some bike, and some drive—it's not a cult or religious rite but all arrive at a water-aerobics class held at Jai's house, with its beautiful perennial borders, rose arbors, and Olympic-size pool on the waterfront off a quiet street in Bellport Village. This has been a summer ritual for more than twenty-five years.

Jai Imbrey and her husband Bob Apfel have also lent their house for many local benefits. Their weathered, shingled house, with pale blue shutters and a stone terrace, located off the rolling lawn to the bay is a sought-after location for social gatherings, just as it was at the turn of the last century when it was known as the Suffolk Country Club. Today, the original row of guest rooms on the second floor is filled with their daughters and friends, and the pool and their boat at the dock below are always busy on the weekends. Classic white canvas umbrellas are opened, seasoned teak lounge chairs are moved for sun or shade, and guests know where to find the baskets of suntan lotion and towels. A round table at the end of the terrace with chairs pulled up makes for a relaxing lunch or drink spot before dinner. When she is not entertaining, Jai can usually be spotted in her garden, snipping, weeding, and watering the foxgloves and the terraced steps filled with fragrant herbs and pots of this season's flowering annuals.

PREVIOUS PAGES: The facade of Jai Imbrey and Bob Apfel's nineteenth-century house faces the bay, and an herb-planted garden located along the stone steps creates a fragrant path to the pool and the bay. RIGHT: The boardwalk through sea grasses to their boat is magical. Simple board railings along the walkway keep the native grasses in line.

ABOVE: Border gardens of old-fashioned flowers, from lavender to foxgloves, are planted around the perimeter of the house. Big white market umbrellas on the stone terrace provide shade for the old wood chaises longues with their white canvas cushions. **OPPOSITE**: New Dawn roses sprawl over the white-painted trellis at the main doorway, and the pale blue and white painted benches provide a shady spot to keep sun hats, suntan lotions, beach towels, and cool drinks.

OPPOSITE: On the shaded front lawn, a sturdy old tree is the perfect location for an old-fashioned swing. ABOVE: The lawn rolls down to the stone-edged pool and the dock.

VILLAGE LIFE

OPPOSITE: Behind the iconic Bellport gate and privet hedge, a nineteenth-century weathered Shingle–style house has dark green shutters, white columns and doors, and a mossy brick path.

A RELAXED RETREAT

Bruce Pask brought his fashion expertise, with his classic American style and love of textiles and textures, to furnishing his home in Bellport Village. With a bit of Scandinavia, a touch of mid-century modern, and a natural color palette, the interiors complement his weekend wardrobe of old khakis, white sneakers, and soft denim jackets. Weekend life revolves around the beach and filling his vintage Volvo with farm stand produce for big buffet suppers out in the barn with friends. Summer rituals also include boat rides to the beach with his partner, Joey, friends, and family members. His twin brother, set designer Scott Pask, had some influence over his decisions while updating this 1920s wood-shingled cottage surrounded by an iconic privet hedge. The Bellport house has been the inspiration for Bruce's curated menswear shop at Bergdorf Goodman. It is designed with wood and warmth, and brings nature and greenery into the space to showcase his personal style.

With a hectic schedule that includes traveling internationally and living and working in New York City during the week, he retreats to this cottage in Bellport to recharge and restore—just an hour-and-a-half away, but another world entirely.

PREVIOUS PAGES: A wall of blue hydrangeas against Bruce Pask's white barn say summer in Bellport. OPPOSITE: Hydrangeas and vines, the perfect plantings for this classic Long Island weathered-shingle house, hug the shingles. Bruce keeps a few vintage Schwinn bikes for a relaxed way of getting around, seeing friends, and stopping for provisions.

ABOVE: Postcards, clippings, and tear sheets of favorite images wallpaper the powder room, making this tiny space a memorable one. **OPPOSITE:** Out in the barn, whitewashed walls are the backdrop for a black-and-white poster collection, and a ladder takes guests up to a bed under the eaves. The long table covered with a drop cloth does double duty, serving as a place for sit-down dinners as well as a bar for larger gatherings when pushed against the wall.

ABOVE: Reclaimed wood planking creates natural pattern and texture as well as a backdrop for the traditional headboard in Bruce's bedroom. He has added chic furnishings from Ilse Crawford's Sinnerlig collection at Ikea, including a bench and a side table, both topped in cork. **OPPOSITE**: Vintage finds from estate sales and art representing his former career as a fashion editor reflect Bruce's personal style for home in his barn.

SUMMER STYLE

WHEN THE WEATHER WARMS UP, a range of whites and summer blues feel right, whether it's in paint colors or cushion covers. The seasonal color palette in nature always informs what we'd like in our own homes and gardens, especially in summer, and the homes in Bellport and Brookhaven hamlet are great examples. The pale blue in a porch ceiling, the painted white picket fences and gates, and the soft, natural color of crushed-shell driveways are just right here. The fresh fragrance and crisp green of privet hedges create outdoor garden rooms and privacy. Summer gardens of lavender and daisies, pink peonies and roses, and trellises by the sea are what work best here. Even the bright pink and tangerine zinnias and yellow sunflowers are a natural appearance in a summerhouse for those who like a more colorful approach.

IT'S NICE TO PUT AWAY THE SHEEPSKINS, wool blankets, and cashmere throws and replace them with cotton and linen sheets, pillow covers, and throws for cooler nights—changes that announce the new season. Even heavy rugs can be rolled up and put away to leave bare wood floors that make sweeping the sand out much easier, or they can be switched out for straw or sisal rugs that have a lighter feeling for the barefoot days. And lighter window treatments such as sheers to shade from the sun and not block the views make sense.

THE SLAM OF A SCREEN DOOR or whirring of a fan brings us right back to childhood, along with the long summer days on the porch or out in the backyard under the shade of a tree.

BEDROOMS IN BLUE AND WHITE, porches with natural wicker furniture, and outdoor tables left bare or dressed in cotton and linen and lit with candles reflect the relaxed style of summer, whether you are by the sea or not. Certain decorating traditions make sense here as they do on Cape Cod or Nantucket, and in old sea captains' houses in other settings by the sea.

OPPOSITE: Classic blue and white awning stripes are a welcoming summer touch, whether in a nineteenth-century sea captain's house in town or a modern beach house on the waterfront.

A FRAGRANT GARDEN

Behind a stately hedge and gate on a quiet cul de sac in Bellport Village lies a maze of outdoor gardens organized by privet hedges. This is the vision and realization of art collector and gardener Charles-Antoine Van Campenhout, who lived here and designed the gardens several years ago. His legacy is now enjoyed and cared for by the new owners, who are also European with a sympathetic aesthetic and who spend their summers here away from their hectic city life. As the seasons unfold, the plantings, perennials, and flowering trees and shrubs come into their own, with magnolias, roses, and peonies in the summer and a boxwood border defining the brick path to the front door. There is a secluded pool area, a kitchen garden, and paths to flowering fruit trees and roses, the top note in any fragrant garden.

The open front porch, with its majestic columns, has seating areas on either side. A soft daybed of pink-striped awning cloth with a canopy and pillows is a perfect place to nap or read, as is the pair of white Adirondack chairs with footrests. There are benches throughout, and dining tables and chairs on the terrace and by the pool, sited for vistas of the gardens while entertaining. The fragrance of the old-fashioned flowers adds to the enchanting ambience.

PREVIOUS PAGES: Behind the stately columned white house are Charles-Antoine Van Campenhout's beautifully designed gardens. OPPOSITE: An overscale European beech hedge creates a dramatic entry to the front of the house, with a brick path and a border of lavender and peonies.

A pool is located behind hedges, which provide a beautiful backdrop and privacy.

ABOVE: A pretty blush canvas daybed welcomes guests to the brick terrace at the front of the home. **OPPOSITE**: Grassy paths through borders and gardens create wonderful walks throughout the property. Along the way, one can glimpse the various garden rooms.

INSPIRATION FROM THE PAST

Architect Elizabeth Roberts was the right person to renovate this cedar-shingled house, where she brought the past and present together in keeping with Bellport's historic district guidelines. It sits naturally among other homes of this late nineteenth-century style, but the interior has been updated in modern-family style. She has transformed many historic houses in Brooklyn, where she lives and works when not in Bellport, and is known for her sensitive renovations for those with young families. Her passion, as well as her firm's specialty in adapting and reusing old buildings, was just the thing to bring to this house in historic Bellport Village, where Elizabeth and her husband, New York City physician John Michael McKnight, and their young son and dog, have made a home. She has retained a lot of the original fabric of this circa-1850s house, with its beadboard ceilings, wood-planked floors, period fireplaces, and old double-hung windows. But spaces were opened up, and a pool and screened garden house were added to the back, always ready for drinks and dinner parties in summer.

PREVIOUS PAGES AND OPPOSITE: The small screened porches upstairs and downstairs in Elizabeth Roberts and John Michael McKnight's home have wood trim, which has weathered with the house's shingles. The trim is a soft gray. The pool is a major addition to their property.

OPPOSITE: The inside dining room also doubles as a playroom, and has a built-in banquette with storage sections underneath, perfect for their son's toys and games. ABOVE: For the living room, Elizabeth kept the original windows, painted the fireplace to make it the focal point, and filled the space with a mix of casual furnishings.

RIGHT: Bedrooms show the same mix of past and present as everything else throughout the house, with whitewashed horizontal paneling, period radiators, modern beds, and practical reading lamps at their sides. **FOLLOWING PAGES**: Peg racks for hanging up clothes and hats have been added to several walls.

ABOVE: Outdoor decking and a wood pergola connect the main house with the new garden structure. **OPPOSITE**: The interior wood has been left natural. Supports open up the ceiling height and provide a design element that makes the old look new.

A CLASSICAL APPROACH

The clean white mailbox by the driveway is the first clue. A simple design yet it's just right, making you look at the pea-gravel driveway (the material of choice here) and the white-shingled house stripped of any unnecessary detail. Brian Sawyer is a principal of Sawyer-Benson, a New York City architectural firm that is the choice of those in-the-know in The Hamptons and the city, bringing some of the oldest estates and town houses back to their original glory and building new houses that work seamlessly with the landscape.

Brian's weekends, though, are about creating his own environment, seen here respecting the architecture of the past and integrating his own aesthetic throughout the house and gardens. The property that surrounds this house has become his palette. He has painted his interiors in subtle shades of off-white, and planted gardens with pale roses and lilies. Built in the early 1900s, the house was the local parsonage, and its original use is reflected in the layout of the public spaces and guest rooms as well as the outbuildings that Brian is reinterpreting as his outdoor garden rooms and spaces for entertaining.

PREVIOUS PAGES: Brian Sawyer's nineteenth-century house is surrounded by lush plantings and flowering shrubs. The charming backyard includes a trellised spot for lounging and dining.
OPPOSITE: A screened porch provides shelter from the summer sun, and the slam of the screen door takes you back to the house's early days. The grid trellises are covered with fragrant old-fashioned roses.

PREVIOUS PAGES: The serene living room doesn't need any window treatments. A straw rug and simple white sofas flank the white-painted period fireplace.
RIGHT: Brian opened up the kitchen to accommodate a sink counter with open shelving for easy access to cookware and serving pieces. The counters and floors are all painted pale gray and the cabinetry and shelving soft white. The tall hutch doubles as a bar for entertaining.

ABOVE: An unframed watercolor of three figures at the beach by local artist Gary Clevidence has been placed on the mantel. OPPOSITE: A "shoes-off upstairs" house rule makes sense when visiting the guest bedrooms, all made up with crisp white sheets and bedding, light-finished floors, pale straw rugs, and simple night tables.

WEEKEND GARDENERS

Three-day weekends are the vacation of choice for Ted Kamoutsis and his husband, Mario Rodriguez. They leave the city Thursday evenings so that they can be up and at it early Friday morning, weeding, planting, trimming, and tending to their self-made gardens surrounding their eighteenth-century saltbox. Once Ted and Mario finished restoring and furnishing the interior of the house, with its period paneling and fireplaces, they turned to the outside. And they now have a pickup truck to haul potting soil and trees home. Although they do buy some plants and soil, they pride themselves on dividing plants to extend them, composting and saving all the stones they dig up to reuse for stone paths. It is all very natural and in perfect harmony with their wood-shingled house, barn, and a screened pavilion they use for summer entertaining or a lie down after a strenuous day's work in the garden. Friends who are familiar with the blooming cycle of the gardens are welcome to bring a bucket and shears to cut their favorite peonies, daisies, cornflowers, or lavender to take home and enjoy.

PREVIOUS PAGES: The layout of Ted Kamoutsis and Mario Rodriguez's gardens has been planned to take advantage of paths that meander throughout and wood benches to sit on and enjoy the natural beauty. The perimeter is a mix of trees and shade plantings, including magnolia and myrtle. **OPPOSITE:** The flower gardens are massed with variety and color. Using green and white as the structure throughout, they have created bold sections of the garden in color blocks of lavender and bright yellow that appear at certain times of each season.

AN ALL-GREEN GARDEN

Bellport Lane is a historic district that runs from Main Street to the dock and has shingled houses with white picket fences and deep green-black shutters. Most of them have period gates featuring the iconic Bellport hardware designed by local blacksmith Joseph Shaw and his descendants. This house was built in 1840, and the original stable is now the pool house and guest cottage. Once through the gate, the property is revealed, not as a small lot like its neighboring houses but doubled, with an extensive landscaped tapestry of expansive green lawn and trees, shady paths and terraces, and hidden gardens and borders that extend the outdoor living space. The property was laid out years ago by internationally known landscape architect Edwina von Gal, and owner David Meitus has followed her vision as the garden matured. Plantings have been added and subtracted throughout the seasons. Stone walls and green privet hedges create outdoor garden rooms, and boxwood hedges in rectangular shapes hold the herb gardens. It is here that David and his wife, art dealer Angela Westwater, entertain throughout the summer in style.

PREVIOUS PAGES AND OPPOSITE: David Meitus and Angela Westwater's house is nestled into the all-green garden of shady trees and shrubs—a mix of evergreens and deciduous trees, with under-plantings of myrtle and woodland ferns.

The old carriage house
is now the guest quarters
and includes a party
room for entertaining.
A massive Russian sage
border surrounds the
pool and leads the way
to the new space.

COUNTRY LIVING

OPPOSITE: A vintage red Land Rover built for rugged terrain makes its way easily to the beach over back roads and pathways.

THE OAKS

Set back from the road in a parklike property with a rolling lawn surrounded by shade trees, this cedar-shake Victorian house has been brought back to life by fashion designer Chris Benz, who is known professionally for his love of color and pattern. This is his weekend home, where he entertains, relaxes, gardens, and raises chickens—a very different lifestyle from in the city. Incorporating a love for historical architecture with a modern sensibility, Chris's home is layered with colorful pillows and quilts, throws and blankets, and rugs and trimmings. Walls are covered with an eclectic mix of drawings, prints, paintings, and portraits collected from galleries and flea markets over the years or just found online. Inside, he has retained the period fireplaces and wood moldings, the beadboard ceilings, and the finials on newel posts. Large, gilt-framed landscapes and mirrors are right at home here along with Chinese porcelain lamps and period wicker chairs. Chris prefers to use one rich color as the background in each room and then spice it up with texture in furniture and accessories.

The house, known as The Oaks, is a rambling three-story dwelling with wraparound porches and landings, nooks and crannies, and quirky outbuildings for potting and raising chickens. It was built in 1886 by distinguished local philanthropist Thomas J. Morrow. Chris grew up spending summers in his grandparents' nineteenth-century Victorian house on the West Coast, and he fell in love with this one on the East Coast, creating a warm and welcoming retreat.

PREVIOUS AND FOLLOWING PAGES AND OPPOSITE: Shopping online for furnishings with a discerning eye is an enjoyable and time-saving activity for Chris Benz. He has found wonderful treasures from high-end antiques shops to the Salvation Army to furnish his house with.
FOLLOWING PAGES: The dining room's deep tonal walls and trim and creamy ceiling accentuate the Victorian woodwork around the doors and windows.

ABOVE: Because of his love of pattern and color, Chris has painted the walls in a bright palette, with contrasting white ceilings and trim. OPPOSITE AND FOLLOWING PAGES: Chris has created cozy seating areas throughout the house. There are also several guest rooms. With a full house at the height of summer, there are places inside and out for everyone to find a comfortable spot.

ABOVE AND OPPOSITE: One can relax with a book or enjoy a cold drink in one of the screened porches. Since he was young, Chris always wanted chickens, and spent summers with his grandparents in a similar Victorian house. He built a chicken coop like his screened porches and lets the chickens roam around the garden during the day.

SUMMER GUESTS

BELLPORT AND BROOKHAVEN HAMLET are the kind of places that people like to visit. The relaxed pace, the seaside setting, the nineteenth-century houses, and the small-town feel make them a destination all year round, but especially when the weather is warm and the sun is shining. And friends here welcome other friends' guests, so drinks and dinner parties are always interesting and include a good mix of friends, old and new.

SOME GUESTS HAVE STANDING HOLIDAY WEEKENDS to visit, some come for local events of interest, and some come for a last-minute invitation. I like to have guest rooms at the ready in case a friend or two stops by and stays. Keeping it simple is the key: let people know where things are and tell them to make themselves at home. There are always extra towels for the beach, and a stack of magazines and beach reads in the rooms. Water bottles, suntan lotion, straw hats, and shawls are in easy-to-find places; there are plenty of quiet spots around the house for reading; and napping on a porch or deck, in the shade of a tree, or tucked in the dunes at the beach is encouraged. Guest rooms should have a comfortable chair to read in, throws, extra pillows, and a good reading light. A table or desk is important for laptop or iPad sessions, and a scented candle, matches, and a water carafe and glass make a stay more comfortable. A folding luggage rack in the bedrooms, extra hangers in the closets, and hooks or Shaker peg racks behind bedroom and bathroom doors make it easy to keep casual

clothing and towels in order. I always leave fresh guest soaps and tissues in the bathrooms and add a simple bouquet of wildflowers to make it feel like summer.

BREAKFAST IS EASY TO PUT TOGETHER, with coffeepot and teakettle ready and granola, fruit from the farm stand, and breads and jams laid out for early risers to fix for themselves. It's more enjoyable to cook with friends, so I always say "yes" to offers of help in the kitchen. Children love to set the table, so I like to press them into service, teaching them a bit about the basics of place settings along the way. Writing or drawing place cards or menus is a great project for artistic friends and children, and there are always fun results from these collaborations.

OLD-FASHIONED BOARD GAMES like Scrabble or Trivial Pursuit are also great to keep on hand for those rainy days or long evenings. Keeping a Wi-Fi password and any log-in information for streaming services like Netflix on display is a good idea, too. Being a vintage film fan, I have a library of old movies and subscribe to all the British film rental services. A summer weekend is a perfect time to show an old movie projected on the side of the house, or on strung-up sheets, with lawn chairs out and friends and neighbors invited to the show—it always creates a sense of occasion and an evening to remember. Local summer events are always fun for guests, too, from a Fourth of July parade, to a sidewalk art show, to an auction or a farm stand visit, to a yard sale or a church bake sale.

OPPOSITE: A row of informal straw slippers invites houseguests to use them while visiting—a nice summerhouse touch.

AN ENGLISH COUNTRY HOUSE

It was love at first sight when Camilla and David Gallacher first saw this circa-1910 house behind a long, white stucco wall. The house and grounds were expansive enough for their family—which included young twin boys—to grow into. But it needed updating, and Camilla knew just what she wanted to do. They moved into this house in Brookhaven hamlet from London after living and working a few years in Manhattan. What was meant to be a weekend retreat soon became their full-time home.

The dining room, with its paneled walls and ceiling, was converted into a kitchen. Navy blue cabinets at the base of the kitchen's island and a thick butcher-block countertop make this an inviting and practical space. Throughout the house, architectural details were preserved: the wood newel post to the stairway has a new sea grass runner; and batten walls in the sitting room were painted. A row of practical hooks for jackets and dog leashes has been installed. The carriage block outside the stucco wall was given a fresh coat of paint. These days, it is used to mount a bicycle instead of a horse.

Camilla loves to cook and has an appreciative audience in the neighborhood. She is always ready to make a cup of tea and welcome friends out for a walk. The updated look of the house and personal style of the owners make it feel as if one has walked into an English country house in Hampshire.

PREVIOUS PAGES: The Gallacher family's early twentieth-century house's expansive backyard now includes an idyllic pool with an arbor for shade. OPPOSITE: The entry, adjacent to the kitchen, is painted Blackberry with floors in Newburyport Blue, both by Benjamin Moore. This is where boots and dog leashes are stored for the next outing. In summer, coats and scarves are replaced with a collection of straw hats.

ABOVE AND OPPOSITE: In a corner of the living room, sheepskins soften vintage chairs, and a collection of art includes a print of a Land Rover by neighbor and artist Hugo Guinness. The walls here are painted Baby Seal Black by Benjamin Moore.

Designed by Camilla, the extra-long kitchen island is ideal for entertaining, with a copper kettle always at the ready. To retain the one-hundred-year-old paneled walls and ceiling, she created this practical island, painted in Farrow & Ball's Railings, with a thick butcher-block counter that also doubles as a potting and flower-arranging area. The white walls throughout are painted in Steam by Benjamin Moore. A painting of Camilla's godmother keeps her company in the kitchen.

ABOVE AND OPPOSITE: The bedroom is also a study in navy blue and white, but here especially, in the textiles Camilla collects and uses throughout the house. Artwork by Hugo Guinness is included in the mix.

ABOVE: A shaded area of the porch, with whimsical rattan chairs and bamboo lanterns, is a welcoming back entry to the house and the adjoining brick patio. **OPPOSITE, TOP**: The nearby Hamlet Organic Garden, locally known as the HOG Farm, sells bunches of wildflowers throughout the season. Camilla can't resist filling her bicycle basket with them to create bouquets at home for table settings and guest rooms. **BOTTOM**: Camilla has created a raised-bed kitchen garden of herbs and tomatoes, safe from roaming rabbits and deer.

ABOVE AND OPPOSITE: The brick patio outside the kitchen is now an outdoor dining area and living space, with comfy seating and pillows under the shade of the trees where Camilla and her dog, Margo, spend sunny days arranging wildflowers.

SOMETHING OLD, SOMETHING NEW

Longtime friends and house transformers, John Guidi and Keith Pollock fell in love with this classic late nineteenth-century Shingle-style house and outbuildings, seeing the potential for a great project. With interesting structural detailing and old beams and fireplaces already in place, they opened the house up, resurfaced floors and walls, and filled it with their collections of furniture, lighting, artwork, and accessories—treasures found online and at local antiques shops, auctions, and estate sales—and made it their own. The exterior has been restored with respect to its 1870s character, and it is a pleasant surprise to enter the newly opened-up spaces in the interior. Once small, dark rooms are now spacious and light-filled, with newly designed fireplaces, wood stoves, and comfortable upholstery. Beams and beadboard have been reinterpreted, leaky windows and doors tightened up, and furnishings with provenance placed just so to create a sophisticated interior that reflects John and Keith's point of view for their lifestyle in the country.

PREVIOUS PAGES: The tonal color palette and painted ceiling beams in the living room of John Guidi and Keith Pollock's late nineteenth-century house makes a small space appear larger.
OPPOSITE: A corner has taken a decidedly modern turn, with a floating console and a wood lamp on top. A bonsai tree sits on a found wood end table, now a plant stand.

The now modern, sculpted fireplace surround is the focal point of the living room. The house is filled with art and found objects collected along the way. The painting on the left of the fireplace is by John's sister, artist Jennifer Guidi.

ABOVE: The paint treatment of the period stairway, the steel gray sisal runner, and a modern light fixture bring new life to this area. OPPOSITE: A great room has been carved out of the old carriage house, now a guesthouse. They kept the brick floor and ceiling beams, but with fresh paint and new furnishings it has become a go-to place for entertaining. The chairs are Guillerme et Chambron, the table was custom made for the space, and the sofa is Vico Magistretti.

A classic Ikea kitchen has taken on a new life in matte black with granite cladding and backsplash. A modern wooden shutter treatment in lacquered white lets light in and also allows for privacy. And the natural wood floating shelving unit, inspired by architect Charlotte Perriand, takes the place of traditional kitchen cabinets.

THE POND PEOPLE

Driving along Beaver Dam Road in Brookhaven hamlet, there is always time to slow down and look at the pond, with its life-size leaves and changing seasonal palette in the surrounding gardens—but especially in the summer, when life here revolves around the blooming of the lilies in the pond. Dinners and lunches are planned with a view, either on the lawn or under the pergola of wisteria—this is summertime in the hamlet.

Everyone in the neighborhood, young and old, knows just who Tom Cashin and Jay Johnson are: "The pond people!" They started with a modest Cape Cod–style house as a weekend home many years ago and then, about ten years ago, acquired the adjacent property with the pond. They integrated both properties and started gardening and planting with the pond as a focal point, then decided that the small house there needed to be expanded, too. Pretty soon, the new guesthouse was larger than the original house and they fell in love with it and moved into it as their main residence, calling it The Lily Pad. All the while, the gardens were expanding and maturing, and Jay was in his element as the head gardener. As principals of a well-known interior design firm and textile company in New York City, Tom and Jay are at ease in the world of design, and they have imbued their own home with the colors and textures of their art, Arts and Crafts furniture, and collections they have acquired over the past forty-plus years of living and traveling together. Their home is their own personal work of art; their gardens are enjoyed by all in the community.

PREVIOUS AND FOLLOWING PAGES AND OPPOSITE: Tom Cashin and Jay Johnson love to entertain, and of all the places to gather friends on their property, none is more magical than the long table set in the pergola draped in purple wisteria. The majestic leaves in the lily pond keep friends in awe over their size.

BARN LOVE

When Isabella Rossellini found this property, a few acres in the woods at the end of a quiet road in Bellport Village, she called on her architect friend Pietro Cicognani to help her with it. With their vision, they turned an old red barn on the land into a home, updated an existing cottage for guests, and built a new structure with a pool and sauna. Simple farm fencing was installed to keep the dogs and chickens on the property and other animals out, and paths were defined to make sense of the buildings in the compound. Wildflowers were planted, a firepit dug, and the result was the family home she always wanted. A little bit of Swedish influence, a little bit of Italian style, it is a place to slow down in between her international travels: acting, producing shows, being a spokesperson for Lancôme's beauty and makeup products. In summer, there are twinkling lights in the central garden, where friends and family visit over drinks, and when it's cooler they gather around a big table in the barn for family-style dinners. An invitation to Isabella's barn means an evening to remember, with delicious food and Italian wines; a mix of friends, family members, and neighbors; and conversations dipping in and out of Italian, French, and Swedish, with an Australian accent here and a British accent there. And one usually leaves with a box of beautifully colored eggs from her heritage chickens.

PREVIOUS PAGES: Isabella Rossellini's idyllic property at the edge of the woods of Bellport Village includes her home—a restored barn—guest cottage, and an indoor pool pavilion. OPPOSITE: First the heritage chickens arrived, then came runaway pigs named Boris and Pepe, and now there are sheep named after her favorite women artists. She is holding Kahlo, a nod to Frida Kahlo. The others are called O'Keeffe, Duse, Stein, and Garbo. Isabella's country life centers around Mama Farm, the farm she started and runs with the help of her daughter, Elettra. In between international shows she produced and acted in, Isabella finished her master's degree in animal husbandry, wrote a book about chickens, and has installed beehives on her farm. She has expanded the farm with acres for growing the best organic vegetables and flowers, and it's where she hosts concerts, benefit dinners, and screenings for the community.

OPPOSITE AND ABOVE: In the Swedish tradition the wood-clad buildings are stained in a classic barn red, pathways are paved with crushed pebbles, and the fields are filled with wildflowers, adding to the natural beauty of the setting. Old iron cauldrons are planted with seasonal flowers and salvaged garden furnishings are scattered about the property. **FOLLOWING PAGES**: Isabella's working farm is nearby. Here, the sheep graze happily on a misty morning.

WHERE THE PAST MEETS THE PRESENT

Located in Brookhaven hamlet, a once traditional two-hundred-year-old weathered house with a warren of small, dark rooms has been opened up to bring in light and a view of the garden. Design journalist Andrea Codrington Lippke and her husband, photographer Ira Lippke, took on the challenge with the help of friend and architect Jeremy Linzee. With great respect for the period wood beams, original wide-plank floors, and rustic fireplaces, they created a large open space for the kitchen and dining room downstairs, which opens out to a patio and pool for contemporary summer living. Upstairs, tiny bathrooms are now filled with sunlight and big, open showers have been added under new, carefully placed skylights. An unused space has become a playroom for the family, with books, art supplies, toys, and cushions, all you need to construct a fort.

The move here from a spacious Brooklyn loft informed some of the couple's design decisions, and before long, Ira stopped commuting and turned the back guest cottage into a state-of-the-art office. Andrea carves out time to go to the library down the road to work on a new novel when their young children, Rye and Soren, are at school. And they have become involved in the community—at the organic farm, local art gallery, and summer stock theater—to discuss ideas of the day with the many friends here who also left the city. They are here to stay and have named their home Eastward Springs, after a favorite Gerard Manley Hopkins poem.

PREVIOUS PAGES AND OPPOSITE: The locus of Andrea and Ira Lippke's traditional two-hundred-year-old house is the 10-foot-long kitchen island where their children, Rye and Soren, play and do homework while meals are being prepared. Ira and architect Jeremy Linzee designed cabinetry with an Italian firm, GD Cucine. The color was custom matched to the Bleu de Savoie stone counters. They selected Gaggenau stainless steel appliances and a VOLA brass faucet.

PREVIOUS PAGES AND LEFT: The neutral palette in the living room, as well as throughout the house, is the backdrop for the colorful art and photography the couple collects. Simple Scandinavian blonde wood furniture and finishes are a nod to Andrea's heritage and work well with the rustic beams of the original part of the house, built in 1830.

ABOVE: A simple platform bed sits against a cube-shaped structure in the open space. It was created to enclose the new bathroom, which is shown on page 189. **OPPOSITE**: A Danish modern cabinet brings another mid-century element to the design.

ABOVE AND OPPOSITE: Always of interest when touring this house are the bathrooms. The downstairs bathroom has a modern, oval white soaking tub, and the upstairs main bath includes a walk-in shower and full skylight.

ARTISTS' RETREATS

AT HOME WITH THE PAST

Formerly known as the Nelson House, this structure, which is based on traditional Long Island designs, was built in 1931 and had a second story added in the 1960s. About three years ago, writer and editor Trish Hall and her husband, artist Larry Wolhandler, discovered this summerhouse and made it their own.

This couple has a long history of saving old houses and renovating them for today's lifestyle, and this one is their latest accomplishment. A new circular driveway was put in, gardens were established, and the layout of the rooms was reconfigured to accommodate a large open kitchen with a window seat. Although Trish has her quiet corners to read and write in and Larry has his painting studio in the backyard, the heart of the home is the kitchen, where they gather to cook and entertain.

Local landscape gardener John Beitel worked with Trish, who is the gardener in the family, to plan the patio, cutting and herb gardens, and the pool and pergola. Shutters are painted the same white as the shingled exterior, new standing seam copper roofs are installed over the porches, an old Windsor bench is situated for visitors, and there is a pile of seasoned firewood for cool evenings. Floors are all stained, and the stairway has a sisal runner. Now friends stop by to call into the house through the open Dutch door during the summer.

PREVIOUS PAGES: With a unifying coat of white paint inside and out, Trish Hall and Larry Wolhandler's Colonial Revival home has taken on a new life. OPPOSITE: The house has even inspired Larry's new collection of paintings, *The White Series*. A shed in back of the property, which Larry has transformed into his studio, now anchors the pool and pergola.

RIGHT: Trish and Larry have created a new kitchen wing that opens out to a patio with outdoor seating.
FOLLOWING PAGES: Nearby, a cutting garden for flowers and herbs is organized by low stone walls.

A STUDY IN BLACK AND WHITE

A light-filled house and studio on a country road in Brookhaven hamlet is the sanctuary of performance artist Lia Chavez, her husband, digital trend forecaster David Shing, and their young daughter, Ocean. With its simple black exterior and glossy white interior, this suburban ranch has been transformed into a minimalist open-plan space, the setting for meditation, performance rehearsals, and artistic salons this couple is known for hosting in the neighborhood. The former two-car garage entrance is now in the back of the house and rolls up to reveal a large studio and extension of the house living space. Simple narrow shelves placed along walls display the newest design publications, and a large white table and chairs that function as a desk area appear to float on the white epoxy floor. The Italian minimal kitchen keeps appliances and pantry storage hidden behind touch-latch doors. Dining space and bedrooms are also lacquered in an icy white with bright lights, and are filled with carefully curated art and furnishings. The house is a backdrop for their lives, and their salon invitations are sought after by the artistic community members living in the area.

PREVIOUS FOUR PAGES: Lia Chavez and David Shing's light-filled ranch house includes a large studio that was previously the garage. OPPOSITE, TOP: A walnut-base island by Effeti Cucine is the heart of the kitchen. The white window frames a view of the serene backyard, including deck and pool. BOTTOM: In keeping with the design throughout the house, visual distractions are kept to a minimum. A glowing orb light by Jasper Morrison floats over the white table and molded chairs, and a large wall painting by Lia brings color and energy to the dining room.

A MODERN SENSIBILITY

Known on Instagram as the #6ftuphouse, the home of artist and art professor Maya Schindler and her mathematician husband Raanan Schul flooded during Hurricane Sandy and was ripe for renovation. The entire house was lifted 6 feet, and Maya designed horizontal fencing to wrap around the house to screen the new posts and storage area underneath. She continued the wood-slatted fencing around the deck so it has a seamless look. Inside, the rafters are exposed and painted, which gives the space more ceiling height. The all-white space has graphic and colorful accents; it is furnished with found mid-century modern pieces and Raanan's black-and-white surfboard, an ode to a favorite Marimekko design. The kitchen is the heart of the home. In the center of the great room, the expansive kitchen island is control central, where Maya works and cooks, keeping an eye on their two young children who might be reading, painting, doing homework, or playing the cello. From the way she's designed their home, to the way she dresses the children and presents meals for family members and friends, every project is a considered work of art.

PREVIOUS PAGES: Maya Schindler and Raanan Schul's house has been raised and reshingled in cedar. Now they call it on Instagram the #6ftuphouse. OPPOSITE: A classic oval dining table with a walnut top by Eero Saarinen is surrounded by a collection of Charles and Ray Eames chairs as well as two Arne Jacobsen Ant chairs.

The original ranch house has taken on a new life with a raised ceiling and exposed beams, all whitewashed to visually expand the space. The kitchen island is the center of activity. It includes plenty of storage and surfaces for cooking as well as for doing homework.

ABOVE: The bedroom furnishings are a blend of rustic elements, including the light fixtures and bed covering, and such modern touches as a Marimekko-patterned surfboard and a Dyson fan. **OPPOSITE:** The library is chock-full of design inspiration—from shelves of architecture and art books, to a trio of George Nelson hanging lamps, to an iconic Charles and Ray Eames chair and ottoman set. **FOLLOWING PAGES:** A set of vintage butterfly chairs with new white covers surrounds a firepit built for cool evenings. The yard has been relandscaped to take advantage of existing trees and the clover-filled lawn, which Maya and Raanan love because they live on Clover Lane.

SUMMER FLOWERS

WHEN SPRING SHOWERS bring May flowers, summerhouses come to life with bounty from local gardens. Formal arrangements look out of place when there are bouquets from local farm stands, Queen Anne's lace and daisies from the fields, or a friend's cutting garden of peonies to visit with your shears.

FOR THE SEASON, window boxes are filled with petunias, and flowering hanging plants on the porch add colors and patterns that are easy to maintain. Even if there is no room or time for a proper outdoor garden, container gardens outside the door—with a selection of potted plants like geraniums, dahlias, or mixed annuals—are a beautiful touch.

BLUE HYDRANGEAS SAY SUMMER on Long Island: in hedges, garden borders, pots by entrances to welcome guests, and big bouquets on tables, or even just as a single blossom in a vase.

A FAVORITE HOSTESS GIFT TO BRING or receive is a bouquet of seasonal flowers for setting in a bedroom or on the porch, and a nosegay of herbs is always welcome for the kitchen or on the dining table as well as a treat to use in cooking.

ALTHOUGH BEAUTIFUL HAND-BLOWN GLASS VASES add a refined decorative touch, a stash of pretty bottles, odd cups, and old-fashioned jelly jars are always good to have on hand to fill with casual flowers and place throughout the house.

OPPOSITE: Whether it's a bouquet of wildflowers from a field or blossoms from a cutting garden or a farm stand, a few ceramic jugs and assorted glass containers are all you need for a bedside table arrangement or a summer lunch centerpiece.

A WRITER'S TREEHOUSE

A wooded property is the setting for this copper-clad two-story writing studio and research library for an architectural historian and author. The homeowner decided that it was the perfect place for her to work, and commissioned New York City architect Andrew Berman to interpret her vision of a modern treehouse—a room of her own.

During a visit to San Francisco, she had fallen in love with the new design of the M. H. de Young Memorial Museum by Herzog & de Meuron. Its natural materials of copper, wood, and stone seemed well suited for her woodland property. So in 2008 Berman replaced an old barn on the site with the studio, situated to take in an idyllic view of a stream through the treetops. The upper level of the pavilion, with a desk for reading and writing and a seating area for watching films, is her dedicated workspace. The shelves that ring the room are filled with fascinating books about great world architecture and history.

At nine sharp every morning, she goes to her "office" where her paperwork remains in the same spot as the evening before, ready to pick up where she left off. And there are no interruptions of daily life or social obligations, which can get especially busy during the summer months. This is a quiet spot, whose only sounds are the trickling of water in the nearby stream, the rustling of leaves on the surrounding bamboo trees, and the chatter of birds. The treehouse is her private peaceful sanctuary, where she has completed five books.

PREVIOUS PAGES: The studio's main room upstairs, which is cantilevered into the woods with expansive views of a stream and bamboo forest, evokes a feeling of being in a treehouse. OPPOSITE: Filled with natural light, the room functions as an office, writing studio, library, and screening room. The interior walls and custom bookcases and window frames are crafted of Douglas fir.

A STUDIO SETTING

On a narrow winding lane in Brookhaven hamlet, an unassuming suburban-looking house is tucked between horse stables, meadows, and summer cottages. But entering the 1970s residence reveals a very different interior: a stylish art gallery and retreat for owner Beverly Allan. After attending art school in New York City, and after stints as a restaurateur and gallery owner, she decided to return to the South Shore of Long Island, where she grew up. These days she has a pickup truck and is as at home in the country as in the city, and can be seen riding her bicycle to the beach or to her husband John's boat.

Beverly found the house and knew its potential, gutting the interior, then creating a loftlike space downstairs. Exposed beams, rough-hewn wood floors, and smooth white walls showcase the art she exhibits to a group of devoted collectors here. She has celebrated local as well as nationally known artists in her collection. Beverly brings together a group of kindred spirits at her home, who wander through the house with glasses of wine, discussing the art as if they were in Soho or Chelsea. Although furnishings are spare and chosen with care, there are playful, personal touches throughout the space.

PREVIOUS AND FOLLOWING PAGES AND OPPOSITE: A 1970s residence has become a retreat and sometime art gallery for Beverly Allan. Flooring throughout is rough planking, and the rustic stairway to the second floor, which is used for exhibits and the guest quarters, resembles a ladder. White track lights along the beams function as ambient lighting as well as illumination for the changing art installations. In the living room **(PAGES 222–223)**, the paintings on the left and back walls are by Peter Halley and Rodney Dickson, respectively; the sculpture is by Virginia Overton. On the guest bedroom wall **(PAGE 225)** hangs a photograph by Bill Jacobson. A leather chaise by Peter Mann and a sculpture by Bill Jenkins fill the space. Even the open kitchen **(PAGES 226–227)** doubles as a gallery space. The three-dimensional wall piece is by Klara Lidén.

LEFT: Kitchen cabinet doors hide collages of cards, notes, illustrations, and snapshots—Beverly's own personal bulletin or mood board. **ABOVE**: The small bathroom has scaled-down fixtures and a mix of old and new touches, including an artistic bath mat and a painting by Andrew Tarlow. **FOLLOWING PAGES**: One of the guest rooms has an open-beamed ceiling and white enamel flooring. It is furnished with pieces from her art collection, including paintings on the back and right walls by Greg Fadell, a string chair and ashtray by C. T. Jasper and Joanna Malinowska, and a work on paper leaning on the wall by Maya Schindler, along with found objects.

SALTINGS

At the end of a dirt road leading to Bellport Bay, hand-painted wood signs tacked to trees read "Saltings," a British term that refers to an area of coastal land that is regularly covered by the tide. This area along the waterfront in Brookhaven hamlet was important in salt-hay harvesting in the nineteenth century, and today, birders refer to this type of environment as birds' habitats. Following the signs to the end of the road, passing cottages tucked into the woods along the way, one finds a magical collection of buildings nestled in the marshland, with one structure located over a bridge to an island at the edge of the bay. It is Michael Ince's world. He was born in the hamlet and has lived here most of his life, sculpting, painting, printing, and creating or reimagining these one-of-a-kind buildings from scrap wood, driftwood, and found objects. A greenhouse, a guesthouse, a tree house, a garden shed, and a work shed all have Michael's imprint on them, influenced by his love of the sea and the ever-present birdlife. Even the main house, with an art studio on the first floor and an upstairs living space, has a spiral staircase with hand-carved railings, church windows, and whimsical hardware throughout. He and his wife, Zabby Scott, live here year-round, sailing and tending to the wild gardens and a white Peking duck called Charlotte that roams the property and is part of the extended family. Friends and neighbors young and old look forward to invitations to visit what they fondly call the "hobbit houses."

PREVIOUS PAGES: Michael Ince and Zabby Scott's whimsical property includes this vine-covered outbuilding, whose shape is informed by found windows and doors. The exterior and roof are clad with carved shingles. **OPPOSITE:** The main house has a delicate arched window, a bit of trellis, board-and-batten panels, and carved trim on the shingles. Weathervanes have been placed on some of the peaked roofs. Pale sage green paint accentuates the exterior trim of the entrance's doors and windows. A wood-burning stove keeps the building snug in winter.

ABOVE: The Marsh House, designed with references to Japan, is found at the edge of the property, reached by paths and bridges that meander from the house to the bay. OPPOSITE: Michael creates his artwork from driftwood, roping, and found objects—expressing his point of view about the natural beauty of his surroundings.

ACKNOWLEDGMENTS

Thank you to all the friends who graciously opened their doors to let me capture their inspiring homes and gardens for *A Summer Place*. It was a pleasure being welcomed by them, and it was hard to choose from the bounty of beautiful places here in Bellport and Brookhaven.

A special thanks to photographer Marili Forastieri, who was a trooper trudging through the marshes amid clouds of mosquitos to get a shot of my house from the shore and enduring long shooting days in the summer heat. To Doug Turshen, whose design is always what I have in mind, and David Huang, for organizing the abundance of material into such a pleasing book, I am indebted. Sandy Gilbert Freidus's insightful editing of this book and meetings in Bellport to brainstorm about this project made it even more enjoyable—thank you. Jeff Weinstein used his virtual red pencil to correct my grammar and too many commas and make suggestions for stronger stories, always with a smile. And special thanks to Bill Steele for coming to the rescue to photograph almost wilting roses, as well as for his friendship.

Many of the homeowners in this book are in the design and lifestyle worlds. They had wonderful existing photography—I appreciate their help in accessing images from some of my favorite photographers.

Finally, this book wouldn't have happened without the support and vision of publisher Charles Miers and the exemplary team at Rizzoli, especially senior editor Sandy Gilbert Freidus, production manager Colin Hough Trapp, and associate director of publicity Jessica Napp. Thank you all!

OPPOSITE: Flagstones are the material of choice for a winding path through the shaded woodland garden along the perimeter of David Meitus and Angela Westwater's property.

PHOTOGRAPHY CREDITS

Gieves Anderson: Pages 15, 154–155, 157–163

Chris Benz: Page 136

Nicholas Calcott: Pages 200–203, 205

Patrice Casanova: Pages 170–172, 174–177

Patrick Cashin: Pages 164–165, 167–169

Michael Fine: Pages 209–213

Tricia Foley: Page 217 (bottom left)

Marili Forastieri: Pages 2–4, 9–11, 13–14, 16–23, 25 (top right, bottom left and right), 26–27, 29–41, 42–43, 45–49, 50–51, 53–65, 67–71, 74–75, 84–85, 87, 90–91, 104–106, 108–116, 118–119, 121–123, 137, 140–142, 144–153, 191–193, 195–199, 206–207, 217 (bottom right), 214–215, 218–219, 221, 239, Back Cover

Howie Guja: Pages 73, 125

Matt Harrington: Pages 78, 80

Marthe Hoet: Pages 222–223, 225–231, 232–234, 236–237

David Land: Pages 126–127, 129–135

Ira Lippke: Pages 178–179, 181–189

Jeff McNamara: Front Cover

Matthew Mead: Pages 25 (top left), 139, 217 (top left, top right), Jacket flap author photograph

Nicolas Mirzayantz: Pages 88–89

Michael Skott: Page 83

Trevor Smith: Pages 76, 81

Eric Striffler: Pages 92–94, 96–103

Bjorn Wallander/Otto: Page 79

First published in the United States of America in 2021 by
Rizzoli International Publications, Inc.
300 Park Avenue South
New York, NY 10010
www.rizzoliusa.com

Copyright © 2021 Tricia Foley
Publisher: Charles Miers
Project Editor: Sandra Gilbert Freidus
Editorial Assistance: Hilary Ney, Dylan Michael Julian, Sara Pozefsky
Design: Doug Turshen with David Huang
Production Manager: Colin Hough Trapp
Managing Editor: Lynn Scrabis

Printed in China

2021 2022 2023 2024 / 10 9 8 7 6 5 4 3 2 1

ISBN: 978-0-8478-7000-4
Library of Congress Control Number: 2020948892

Visit us online:
Facebook.com/RizzoliNewYork
instagram.com/rizzolibooks
twitter.com/Rizzoli_Books
pinterest.com/rizzolibooks
youtube.com/user/RizzoliNY
issuu.com/Rizzoli